First Field Trips

Theater

by Cari Meister

Bullfrog
Books

Ideas for Parents and Teachers

Bullfrog Books let children practice reading informational text at the earliest reading levels. Repetition, familiar words, and photo labels support early readers.

Before Reading

- Discuss the cover photo. What does it tell them?
- Look at the picture glossary together. Read and discuss the words.

Read the Book

- "Walk" through the book and look at the photos. Let the child ask questions. Point out the photo labels.
- Read the book to the child, or have him or her read independently.

After Reading

- Prompt the child to think more. Ask: Have you ever been to the theater? What did you see performed?

Bullfrog Books are published by Jump!
5357 Penn Avenue South
Minneapolis, MN 55419
www.jumplibrary.com

Copyright © 2016 Jump! International copyright reserved in all countries. No part of this book may be reproduced in any form without written permission from the publisher.

Library of Congress Cataloging-in-Publication Data

Meister, Cari.
  Theater / by Cari Meister.
    pages cm. — (First field trips)
  Includes index.
  ISBN 978-1-62031-298-8 (hardcover: alk. paper) —
  ISBN 978-1-62496-364-3 (ebook)
  1. Theater—Juvenile literature. I. Title.
  PN2037.M395 2015
  792—dc23
                                        2015033965

Editor: Jenny Fretland VanVoorst
Series Designer: Ellen Huber
Book Designer: Lindaanne Donohoe
Photo Researcher: Lindaanne Donohoe

Photo Credits: All photos by Shutterstock except: CanStock Photo, 17; Corbis, 6–7, 18–19, 22; iStock, 3, 4, 12–13, 24; Thinkstock,15.

Printed in the United States of America at Corporate Graphics in North Mankato, Minnesota.

Table of Contents

Behind the Curtain 4

At the Theater 22

Picture Glossary 23

Index 24

To Learn More 24

Behind the Curtain

Where is the class going?

To the theater!

It is a place to see plays.

Today we are lucky.
We go in the stage door.
It is for cast and crew.

Everyone gets ready.
The actors put on makeup.

They put on costumes.

Wow! That is a big wig!

The crew checks the set.

Looks good!

Are the props in place?

Yes!

props

set

They test the lights.
The spotlight works.

15

The actors warm up.

They stretch.

16

They sing.

They say lines.

The musicians come.
They sit in the pit.
They warm up, too.

All is ready.

The lights go down.

We take our seats.

It is showtime!

At the Theater

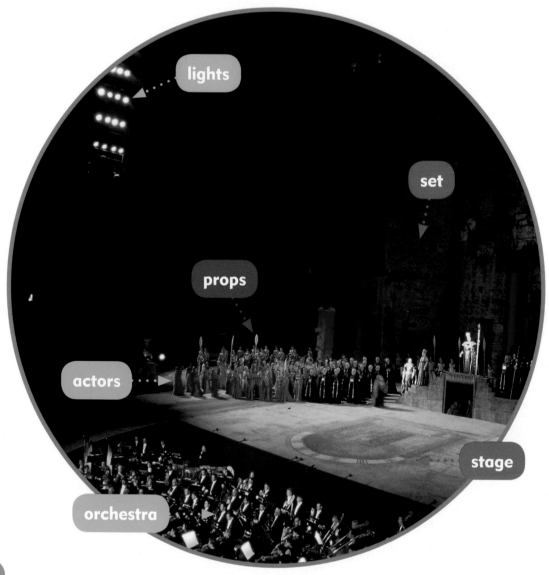

lights

set

props

actors

stage

orchestra

Picture Glossary

costumes
Special clothes worn in order to look like someone or something else.

pit
A sunken area in front of the stage where a theater orchestra sits.

makeup
Colored materials applied to the face to change or improve appearance.

set
The scenery for a play.

musicians
People who play musical instruments.

wig
A covering for the head made of real or artificial hair.

Index

actors 8, 16

cast 7

costumes 10

crew 7, 12

lights 15, 21

makeup 8

musicians 18

pit 18

plays 5

props 12

set 12

warming up 16, 18

To Learn More

Learning more is as easy as 1, 2, 3.

1) Go to www.factsurfer.com

2) Enter "theater" into the search box.

3) Click the "Surf" button to see a list of websites.

With factsurfer.com, finding more information is just a click away.